A Piper's American Odyssey

A Piper's American Odyssey

BOOK ONE

Pipe Major Hugh Macpherson, CD

PENUMBRA PRESS
www.penumbrapress.ca

 Copyright 2006 © Hugh D. Macpherson and Penumbra Press

No part of this publication may be reproduced, stored in a retrieval system or transmitted, in any form or by any means, without the prior written consent of the publisher or a licence from The Canadian Copyright Licensing Agency (Access Copyright). For an Access Copyright licence, call toll free to 1-800-893-5777 or visit www.accesscopyright.ca

LIBRARY AND ARCHIVES CANADA
CATALOGUING IN PUBLICATION
Macpherson, Hugh, 1947-
   A piper's American odyssey. Book 1 [music] / Hugh Macpherson.
H. Macpherson Canadian.
Collection of contemporary bagpipe compositions written by the author and by American composers.
ISBN 1-894131-95-9
1. Bagpipe music. 2. United States — Songs and music. I. Title.
M145.M172 2006   788.4'915990973   C2006-901181-8

Photo of "Polyphemus the Cyclops" on page 17 is a detail of Michele Todini's Harpsichord, supported by Tritons, with gilded gesso relief showing procession of Galatea, c. 1675. All rights reserved, The Metropolitan Museum of Art. The Crosby Brown Collection of Musical Instruments, 1889 (Accession # 89.4.2929).

Facsimile of the painting of Baron von Steuben by Charles Willson Peale c. 1782 on page 48 is courtesy of the Collections of Independence National Historical Park, Philadelphia, Pennsylvania, INDE 14164

Canada

Penumbra Press gratefully acknowledges the financial support of the Government of Canada through the Book Publishing Industry Development Program (BPIDP) for our publishing activities. We also acknowledge the Government of Ontario through the Ontario Media Development Corporation's Ontario Book Initiative.

A987654321

Acknowledgements

I would like to express my appreciation to the people without whom this book would not have appeared.

First, I am grateful to the infinitely patient General John de Chastelain OC, CMM, CD, CH, who always seems willing to find the time to read my stories, doggedly stripping them of excessive adjectives and adverbs while rearranging dyslexic sentences. He is a competent piper and an officer of the old school who understands that loyalty must always go two ways.

I thank another useful piper, Colonel Richard Adams, for his initial inspiring burst of enthusiasm for this project, his steady flow of ideas and improvements, and his careful edits.

I am grateful to the Scottish Tartans Authority for their assistance and permission to use the American Tartan (ITI No. 464) on the cover of this book.

From the very beginning, Mag Carson of Penumbra Press has shown the most impressive forbearance with my abysmal lack of computer skills. She is also responsible for the wonderful drawings of the three Loyalist soldiers of the Queen's Rangers, Royal Highland Emigrants and Butler's Rangers.

Finally, I thank my wife, Susan, who endures the dark-of-the-night musical inspirations, permits the endless hours I spend huddled over a practice chanter or a computer, then suffers with grace through the initial, unedited story reading or tune playing.

— H.D.M.

This book, and the music it contains, is dedicated to the everlasting memory
of our civilian and military relatives, loved ones and friends
murdered at the hands of terrorists on 11 September 2001.

Contents

PART ONE

MODERN AMERICA

PIPE MAJOR HUGH MACPHERSON	Makan Al Ma'asat	Lament	13
	The Forum	March	15
	Arlington Cemetery	Lament	16
	The Cyclops	Air	17
	Pearl Harbor	March	18
	MacArthur's Return	Retreat March	19
	First Sergeant Walter E. Nail	March	20
	Pipe Major Sandy Keith	March	21
	The New York Police Pipers	March	22
	Central Park	March	23
US ARMY FOURTH INFANTRY DIVISION			
	The Toppled Tyrant	March	25
	Iraqi Freedom	Strathspey	26
	Steadfast and Loyal	Reel	27
US ARMY TENTH MOUNTAIN DIVISION			
	Fort Drum	Slow March	29
US MARINE CORPS			
	Shout Semper Fi	March	30
	Fallujah	Hornpipe	31
US AIR FORCE			
	Billy Mitchell	March	33
	Colonel Adams's Bagpipe	Slow March	34

PART TWO

EIGHTEENTH-CENTURY AMERICA

PIPE MAJOR HUGH MACPHERSON	Cape Henry	March	36
	Plymouth Rock	Retreat March	37
	Yearning to Breathe Free	March	37
	Bunker Hill	Slow March	38
	Independence Hall	Strathspey	39
	George Washington's Jig	Jig	40
	Fort Necessity	Strathspey	41
	Brandywine Creek	Reel	43
	Ticonderoga	March	45
	Royal Highland Emigrants	March	46
	Butler's Rangers	Slow March	47
	Die Wandernden Preussen	Slow March	49
	Old Ironsides	Waltz	51
	Yorktown	Reel	52
	The Louisiana Purchase	Strathspey	53

PART THREE

CONTEMPORARY AMERICAN COMPOSITIONS

COLONEL RICHARD ADAMS	Connie Jean	Slow March	56
	Tenor's Delight	March	56
	Patch Barracks	March	57
PIPE MAJOR SANDY KEITH	The 'K' Birl	March	58
JOHN TURNER	Macpherson's Farewell to Croatan	Slow March	59
	Dr. Malcolm Macpherson-Smith	March	59
RAY SCOTT	The Lion's March	March	60
	Rachel's Dance	Hornpipe	60
	Milver's Cheery Day	Hornpipe	61
CHARLIE GLENDINNING	Kip	Jig	62
	The Rookery	Strathspey	63
	The Rosary	Strathspey	63
JOHN RECKNAGEL	Fort Jackson	March	64
	Morangie	Hornpipe	64
	Iain Macdonald-SOBHD	Jig	65
JASON BARTH	Road to Grandfather	Hornpipe	66
	Slash Pine	Reel	66
	The Turncoat	Jig	67
SCOTT BRAINARD	Megan Deeney	Waltz	68
	Pensées	Slow Air	68
	Sideways Down the Highway	Reel	69
	Slip Jig 1991	Jig	69

Foreword

The tragic events of 11 September 2001 shook the world. This collection of pipe music contains a special tribute to those from many countries who lost their lives during the attacks.

The United States and Canada are far more than close allies and trading partners. We have relatives and friends on both sides of the border, and we share similar values, hopes and dreams. The development of both our countries has been greatly influenced by the same European cultures, and we both have historic ties strongly linked to the United Kingdom. In Canada, British piping traditions have long been a part of the national heritage, commemorating significant historical and military events through the composition of pipe tunes. In the United States, where bagpipe music is becoming increasingly a part of American life, there has been little pipe music composed by Americans and even less published formally. I hope this book may ignite a new trend within the American piping community and encourage more American compositions, particularly ones commemorating significant historical events.

I would like to thank Pipe Major Hugh Macpherson and the other composers whose work is presented in this book. Hopefully their music will bring pleasure to all who play and hear it, at the same time reminding us of our history and the sacrifices of those who have made us what we are today.

Paul Cellucci
United States Ambassador to Canada
(April 2001 to March 2005)

PART ONE

Modern America

The Place of Sorrow

In Arabic, the parts of the world where Islam is dominant is called *dar al-Salam* — the place of peace. The rest of the planet is called *dar al-Harb* — the place of war.

Makan al-Ma'asat means the place of sorrow. The three locations where Americans and others died on 11 September 2001 are indeed places of sorrow. Those responsible for the terrorist attacks on that date did not, however, represent all of the people of Islam, which is a religion based on the teaching of peace and hope.

This lament is "Makan al-Ma'asat." It commemorates the victims of 11 September and the many others who have lost their lives since in the defense of peace and freedom and in the fight against terrorism.

Lament **MAKAN AL MA'ASAT** PM H. Macpherson

MM60 (Second and third lines are harmonies — Recommended ratio 3:2:1)

MODERN AMERICA

The Destruction of a Civilization

By the end of the fourth century, European civilization was under constant attack by barbarians determined to capture for themselves the wealth and property of the citizens. Many of those European citizens with the most to lose refused to contribute in kind or in service to the common defense. The army that was supposed to protect them was almost entirely filled with outsiders — "mercenaries" who were expected, between patrols, to grow their own food and to provide future army recruits with the daughters of the local people who lived near their garrisons. Even the officer corps was largely drawn from among the tribal chieftains of these outsiders and had never seen the center of civilization. In too many cases, their personal agenda took precedence over the commonweal.

The city of Rome, although still the center of commerce, education, and culture, had long ceased to be the capital. The scantily defended borders permitted endless incursions by marauders and the "eternal city" itself was finally besieged. On 24 August 410 CE the barbarian leader, Alaric, captured it and turned his men loose for three days of rape, pillage, and burning.

By 476 CE all government control in Europe had been destroyed and for almost a thousand years the continent endured the dark ages: survival of the fittest, starvation, disease, armed raids, and the depredations of warlords and senior churchmen unchecked by any real rule of law.

The author sees very disturbing parallels with the equally barbarous attacks of 11 September 2001, the reaction of our civilization to the attacks, and therefore fears for the future of this civilization.

March # THE FORUM   PM H. Macpherson

Lament # ARLINGTON CEMETERY   PM H. Macpherson
MM60 (Second lines are harmony — Recommended ratio 4:1)

Progressive chord

Progressive chord

Air   # THE CYCLOPS   PM H. Macpherson

Polyphemus the Cyclops

At the Metropolitan Museum in New York City the author found this almost man-sized gilded statue of the anti-social Cyclops who tried to eat Odysseus and his men. In the statue, circa 1675, the Italian artist and inventor Michele Todini had his subject playing a new type of bagpipe similar to one which Todini had just constructed. It has a bellows beneath the right arm and a bag under the left. Fitted into a single large stalk, there are two chanters and a large drone, the latter shaped like a modern saxophone.

March   **PEARL HARBOR**   PM H. Macpherson

Pearl Harbor

Since its emergence as a world power during the Second World War and its development as a prosperous and growing nation, the United States has become the focus of envy, admiration, and enmity. It has long been a magnet for those wishing to flee oppression and seek a new life.

Some outsiders feel that America's championing of democracy worldwide, or its appetite for natural resources, poses a threat to its existence, justifying attacks on the US and on Americans elsewhere. This attitude began with the Japanese attack on Pearl Harbor in 1941 and continues today.

Largely isolationist until 1941, the United States is now the world's only superpower. It remains at the forefront of defending democracy and freedom globally, expending vast amounts of its wealth in doing so.

Retreat March   # MACARTHUR'S RETURN   PM H. Macpherson

General Douglas MacArthur

General Douglas MacArthur (1880-1964) entered West Point in 1898 and graduated at the top of his class four years later. He rose to the rank of brigadier general and commanded the Rainbow Division in France until the end of the First World War. He returned to West Point as superintendent, after which he had various duties in the Philippines.

In 1930 MacArthur was appointed chief of staff of the US Army. Five years laters he returned to the Philippine commonwealth at the request of his friend, leading politician Manuel Quezon. There he oversaw a US mission aiming to catalyze Philippine independence by 1946.

The Japanese attack on Pearl Harbor in December 1941, however, brought the US into war in the Pacific. Shortly after, MacArthur's meager military forces were driven down to the tip of the Bataan Peninsula by overwhelming numbers of Japanese troops, leaving them with no immediate hope of relief. MacArthur was ordered by President Roosevelt to abandon his men and leave for Australia. He did so with a promise — "I will return."

MacArthur held fast to his word; after defeating the enemy's land forces and accepting their surrender aboard the *Missouri* on 2 September 1945, he returned. For the next five years he helped rebuild the shattered Japanese nation, serving as supreme commander of Allied forces in Japan.

March **FIRST SERGEANT WALTER E. NAIL** PM H. Macpherson

First Sergeant Walter E. Nail (Retired)

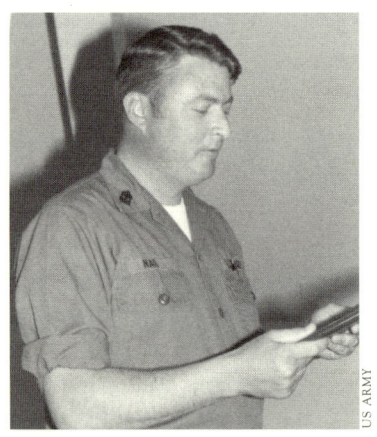

The composer first met Walt Nail upon being posted to West Germany in 1977 to lead Canadian Forces Europe Pipes and Drums. CFE Pipes and Drums was very much in demand all over Europe, and a young and inexperienced pipe major had been "thrown in at the deep end." The help and advice provided by Walt Nail and his beautiful German wife, Beate, was invaluable in making the job a success.

The composer's knowledge of basic harmonic structures, which has permitted experimentation in closed-harmony arrangements for pipe bands, was largely gained from Walt Nail. Later, he provided the composer's daughter, Victoria, with her first trombone when she began her musical education in Canada.

Walt Nail was born in Mississippi and raised in Memphis, Tennessee, where, like millions of other American musicians, he learned his music as part of the wonderful Salvation Army band program. He joined the US Army in 1959, serving 26 years as a military bandsman. Retired in 1985, he now resides in Evans, Georgia.

PIPE MAJOR SANDY KEITH

March — PM H. Macpherson

March   # THE NEW YORK POLICE PIPERS   PM H. Macpherson

New York Police Department

On several occasions after the murderous attacks on the World Trade Center, the composer was impressed by the musical presentation of the New York police officers playing numerous laments at funerals for serving officers and civilian casualties. The performances of the NYPD Pipes and Drums lent truth to the adage from Congreve, "Music hath charms to soothe the savage breast."

March   **CENTRAL PARK**   PM H. Macpherson

Quasar of Central Park

The author always tried to find a mount to ride in every location his army career took him. This resulted in mounted tours in, among other places, the Greek Peloponnesus, the Rockies, Virginia, Egyptian Giza at the pyramids, and Nicosia, Cyprus.

In Nicosia, a camel and his owner had emigrated from the Middle East. He was earning his fodder providing a photo-op for apparently bullet-proof British tourists who abounded. He was discovered just inside the old wall. Once the author was mounted, another piper fetched a bagpipe and decided that the photo should include "The Camels Are Coming." The camel was a piping judge or a Macdonald! The wild gallop that ensued, with the offending bagpipe protected in the rider's one hand, while the other hand fended off the camel's determined attempts, head reversed, to bite off a kilted kneecap, almost bowled over an astonished Cypriot policeman who was directing traffic in the middle of Metaxas Square.

In New York City, at a better address than the author's, Quasar the horse lives in the famous Claremont Stables on the Upper West Side. A well-bred city boy with good friends in the police mounted division, he reads and obeys traffic signals on his way to and from the park.

US Army Fourth Infantry Division

The divisional shoulder patch of four connected ivy leaves is a visual play on words, referring to the roman numeral IV, assigned to the division. The divisional motto is "Steadfast and Loyal."

Originally raised in 1917 as a combat division, the US Fourth Infantry Division served through the end of the First World War and, when the United States finally entered action in 1941, through the Second World War. During this war, four soldiers of the division, including their commander during the Normandy landing on Utah Beach, Theodore Roosevelt Junior, won the highest United States award for conspicuous bravery under fire, the Medal of Honor. Brigadier General Roosevelt died in action one month later of a heart attack.

Returned home and disbanded at the end of the war, the division was reactivated in 1947 as a training division. Four years later, it was redesignated for operational duty. There followed five years of cold-war service around Frankfurt in West Germany. The division was the first of four United States divisions placed in Germany along with British, Canadian, French, and Belgian troops to stem the tide of Communist aggression.

The Fourth Infantry Division fought in Vietnam for almost five years between September 1966 and December 1970, for which eleven members were awarded the Medal of Honor.

The division, with its state-of-the-art equipment, was to have participated in the second invasion of Iraq by coming through Turkey. Instead it entered Iraq as occupation troops in the exceptionally dangerous "Sunni Triangle" near Tikrit.

After one year, the Fourth Infantry Division returned home to Fort Hood, Texas. It was replaced in Iraq by the US Army First Infantry Division.

March # THE TOPPLED TYRANT PM H. Macpherson

Strathspey

IRAQI FREEDOM

PM H. Macpherson

Reel # STEADFAST AND LOYAL PM H. Macpherson

MODERN AMERICA

US Army Tenth Mountain Division (Light Infantry)

The blue background of the divisional shoulder patch and the crossed bayonets represent the infantry. The bayonets form an X. the Roman numeral for the number ten. The powder-keg shape is meant to suggest the explosive power of the division, while the red, white, and blue colors salute the United States.

The author first met members of the Tenth Mountain Division when he was asked to play at a unit officers' dinner at Fort Drum, a massive training base near Syracuse, New York. The friendly hospitality and military professionalism of the division's officers and senior NCOs was impressive and prompted the slow march on the next page, which is suitable not only for pipers but also for the divisional brass/reed band.

The division was created at the end of 1941. The initial unit, called the Eighty-seventh Mountain Infantry Battalion, was formed and recruited through the efforts of Charles Minot Dole, president of the national ski patrol. By 1943, the battalion had become the Tenth Light Division (Alpine). In January 1945, then known as the Tenth Mountain Division, it entered the Second World War in Italy.

In its first combat, the division took Riva Ridge and Mount Belvedere. This was followed by a fighting advance into the Po River valley. For this, PFC John D. Magrath, of East Norwalk, Connecticut, was posthumously awarded the Medal of Honor.

The division finished the Second World War after taking the Italian towns of Riva and Tarbole at the southern end of Lake Garda, which cut off the enemy's escape route through the Brenner Pass. In just 114 days of combat they defeated five enemy divisions.

They were disbanded at Camp Carson, Colorado, in 1945. Many veterans went on to play key roles in the development of skiing in Colorado.

Reactivated in 1948 as a training organization, it provided NATO front-line troops in Germany until 1958, when it was again deactivated.

In 1989, with the end of the cold war, new threats were emerging. The Pentagon identified a need to increase US capacity in the area of light, highly mobile fighting formations. Accordingly, the Tenth Mountain Division (LI) was reactivated at Fort Drum.

Elements of the division have since figured prominently in operations in Kuwait (1991-92), Somalia (1992-94), Haiti (1994-95), Bosnia/Herzegovina (1997-2000), as well as in current missions in Afghanistan and Iraq.

Slow March # FORT DRUM
MM60
PM H. Macpherson

US Marine Corps

US Marine cap badge

The composer served for thirty-three years in Canadian military units modeled after the regimental system that sustained the British Army for more than four centuries — now being debased for inexplicable reasons. Although armchair critics tend to view the system as a form of tribalism, nothing else in two millennia ever proved quite as effective at producing sound fighting troops.

The composer finds the members of the US Marine Corps very similar in attitude and outlook to those of his fellow Commonwealth soldiers. It was, and is, always very easy to work with marines regardless of their rank; their obvious pride in being a "leatherneck" while serving carries on into whatever career follows that experience. Like his former Black Watch and Royal Canadian Regiment colleagues, the attitude, "once a marine, always a marine," is familiar and comfortable.

March — **SHOUT SEMPER FI** — PM H. Macpherson

Hornpipe

FALLUJAH

PM H. Macpherson

MODERN AMERICA

US Air Force

US Air Force cap badge

The United States Air Force was created on 18 September 1947. It was staffed and equipped by the Army Air Corps, which had evolved out of the Army Signal Corps.

Nine months later, the fledgling organization was put on its mettle when the Soviet Union attempted to starve the citizens of West Berlin into submission. The Allies responded with the Berlin Airlift. USAF C-54 cargo aircraft delivered more than five thousand tons of food and supplies per day. When the airlift began, both U.S. and British aircraft utilized the woefully inadequate Second World War air strip at Tempelhof Air Base; later, with the help of the army engineers and thousands of German volunteer laborers, proper runways were constructed at Tegel Airfield.

The Communists, overwhelmed by Allied might, abandoned the attempted blockade in September 1949.

March **BILLY MITCHELL** PM H. Macpherson

Brigadier General Billy Mitchell

Brigadier General
William Mitchell

Billy Mitchell (1879-1936) enlisted as a private in the Spanish-American War. With the help of his his father, a Wisconsin senator, he was commissioned into the Army Signal Corps. In his late thirties, Mitchell became interested in aviation and took private flying lessons. When the US entered the First World War in 1917, Lieutenant Colonel Mitchell was a tireless and effective leader. Promoted to brigadier general by the end of the war, he led nearly 1,500 Allied airmen. In addition to several foreign medals, he earned the Distinguished Service Cross and the Distinguished Service Medal. However, his abrasive character alienated him from his superiors.

After the war, Mitchell continued to aggravate his superiors with public attacks on their attitudes toward war. He was eventually demoted to colonel. Accused of being vain, petulant, and overbearing, Mitchell was prescient, nonetheless, warning in 1926 of a Japanese carrier-based air attack on Pearl Harbor. Issuing numerous scathing public indictments of his superiors — "non-flying officers in Washington who know nothing about airpower yet try to direct its course" — he was court-martialled for insubordination and suspended without pay for five years. He chose to retire, but continued to proclaim the uses of air power as an offensive weapon until his death in 1936.

Slow March — **COLONEL ADAMS'S BAGPIPE** — PM H. Macpherson

Colonel Richard Adams, PhD, USAF (Retired)

The composer first met Rich Adams when the latter was a United States Air Force captain serving at Stuttgart, Germany, in 1978. A competent, hard-working, and conscientious piper, Adams sought and obtained from his USAF superiors permission to play as one of the guest pipers in the volunteer Canadian Forces Europe Pipes and Drums working two hours down the Autobahn at Lahr. Adams met and married his Canadian highland-dancer wife, Heather, who was also a volunteer member of CFE Pipes and Drums at the time.

To the author, Colonel Adams represents all that is great about the United States of America.

PART TWO

Eighteenth-Century America

March **CAPE HENRY** PM H. Macpherson

Cape Henry

The settlers who first attempted to create a British colony in North America landed at Cape Henry on the southeastern shore of Chesapeake Bay on 26 April 1607. Two weeks later, they sailed inland to begin the establishment of Jamestown.

Off this same shore 175 years later, 5 September 1781, French Navy Admiral François Joseph Paul Compte de Grasse defeated a large Royal Navy fleet attempting to relieve the British forces under General Charles Cornwallis trapped by French and American troops at Yorktown.

The "Battle of the Capes" effectively finished the Revolutionary War.

Retreat March   # PLYMOUTH ROCK   PM H. Macpherson

March   # YEARNING TO BREATHE FREE   PM H. Macpherson

Slow March **BUNKER HILL** PM H. Macpherson

MM60 (Second lines are harmony — Recommended ratio 4:1)

38 A PIPER'S AMERICAN ODYSSEY

Strathspey

INDEPENDENCE HALL

PM H. Macpherson

Independence Hall, Philadelphia

The Pennsylvania State House in Philadelphia, construction of which commenced in 1732, was the grandest structure in the thirteen colonies. Here, half a century later, the Declaration of Independence was adopted, the American Constitution was created, and it was renamed Independence Hall. However, after serving as the birthplace of the United States, the iconic building was used for less noble purposes; it was, for instance, once the Philadelphia dog pound.

It suffered numerous architectural insults through time, but was finally restored to the original appearance by the National Parks Service in 1950.

EIGHTEENTH-CENTURY AMERICA

Jig **GEORGE WASHINGTON'S JIG** PM H. Macpherson

Strathspey — **FORT NECESSITY** — PM H. Macpherson

George Washington and the Seven Years War

In 1754 the French held a huge territory centered on the headwaters of the Ohio River. Their main fort was Fort Duquesne, where Pittsburgh now stands. However, the governor of the British colony at Virginia gave certain prominent families of the colony land grants in that territory. He then sent twenty-one-year-old George Washington, lieutenant colonel of the British militia, into the area with 150 troops.

The inexperienced officer, encountering a long-range patrol of French soldiers on 3 July, immediately attacked them and killed their leader, but he foolishly allowed the rest of the patrol to escape back to Fort Duquesne. Realizing his mistake, he ordered a defensive position constructed on the site of the skirmish, humorously naming it "Fort Necessity." Inevitably, a large French force appeared the next day and overwhelmed the Virginians. They were allowed to march out with their weapons and return home.

However, the small action against the colonials so enraged the authorities that the following year they expelled thousands of French Acadians from British-held territories in what is now Eastern Canada, sending most of them to the French Louisiana territory where their descendants are the Cajuns.

Winston Churchill said that little fight on the Ohio also precipitated what American historians call the French and Indian War, which led to the Seven Years War, fought virtually all over the world by all of the major powers of Europe. It pitted Britain and Prussia against France, Austria, Spain, and Russia.

The Battle of Brandywine Creek

A Queen's Ranger

In autumn 1777 General George Washington's Continental army was having a difficult time against British Regular Army units, as well as loyalist militia regiments raised from among the colonists to oppose the rebels. The Americans were badly mauled just southwest of Philadelphia at Brandywine Creek by the Queen's Rangers, a unit recruited in New York, mostly around Westchester and Long Island. Led by John Graves Simcoe, who was later the first lieutenant-governor of Upper Canada, the Queen's Rangers had the advantage over other British troops of green "camouflage" uniforms. At the end of the battle, Simcoe saved Washington's life when he ordered his soldiers not to shoot him and two other escaping American officers in the back. The Queen's Rangers regiment was later disbanded in Nova Scotia.

Following the battle, Washington's Continental army went into cold and spartan winter quarters nearby at Valley Forge, where Prussian mercenary Baron Frederich von Steuben was able to train them into a more effective fighting force.

Reel # BRANDYWINE CREEK   PM H. Macpherson

Fort Ticonderoga

Where Lake Champlain and Lake George join, in what is now upper New York State, between 1755 and 1758 the French built Fort Carillon, "the key to the continent." This water route was always the best passage for troops in the incessant struggle between French North America and the British colonists to the southeast. The fort controlled the narrow choke point between the lakes.

During the Seven Years War, which resulted in the end of French control in North America, the Marquis de Montcalm successfully defended Fort Carillon with 3,800 Frenchmen and Indians against the incompetent British general, James Abercromby, who commanded 15,000 troops. On 7 July 1758, enraged at the death of his friend and second-in-command Lord Howe the day before, Abercromby launched a suicidal frontal attack on the fort. The famed Black Watch, honored that year with the title Royal Highland Regiment, lost 648, killed or wounded. Then, although the defenders had used up nearly all of their ammunition, Abercromby ordered his soldiers to retreat. This was the most spectacular French success of the century, but General Jeffrey Amherst returned the next year and took the fort as part of his three-pronged advance on Quebec. He renamed it Ticonderoga in honor of one of his Indian allies.

Ticonderoga was the site of the first victory of the American Revolution. On 10 May 1775 Benedict Arnold, Ethan Allen and the Green Mountain Boys accomplished a night crossing from Vermont. They surprised a small company of sleeping British soldiers and took the fort. The captured British guns were dragged overland to Massachusetts by Colonel Henry Knox. Placed atop Dorchester Heights, they were used to drive the British from Boston on 17 March 1776.

Arnold built the first US Navy at Ticonderoga. Although eventually overwhelmed at the battle of Valcour Island, he was successful in stopping a vast British force coming from Canada under General Burgoyne. The British were held up until July 1777, thus giving General George Washington time to strengthen and prepare his Continental army.

March   # TICONDEROGA   PM H. Macpherson

March **ROYAL HIGHLAND EMIGRANTS** PM H. Macpherson

The Royal Highland Emigrants

The idea of raising a colonial regiment from veterans of the Seven Years War was proposed before the American Revolution by Lieutenant Colonel Allan MacLeod in Nova Scotia. In January 1775 he and Major John Small were told to raise two battalions of Royal Highland Emigrants, to be uniformed like the Forty-second Black Watch. In 1782 Sir Guy Carleton was appointed colonel and they became a Regular Army regiment as the Eighty-fourth Regiment of Foot.

The First Battalion helped defend Quebec City against Benedict Arnold's siege and thereafter garrisoned Quebec. Major Small's Second Battalion was scattered throughout much of its service. Elements of the battalion fought at Brooklyn in 1776 and then helped garrison New York City, while others accompanied General Leslie to Virginia in October 1780 and participated at the Siege of Charleston and in South Carolina.

The Royal Highland Emigrants were disbanded at the end of the war and the men and their families given land grants in Nova Scotia and Quebec.

Slow March — **BUTLER'S RANGERS** — PM H. Macpherson

Butler's Rangers

Colonel John Butler's Rangers were raised along what is now the New York-Ontario border near Niagara Falls.

They served — together with the New York King's Royal Regiment, commanded by Sir John Johnson — in several border skirmishes and successfully repelled a large Continental army force, led by General Richard Montgomery, bent on forcing Canada to become the fourteenth American ex-colony.

At the end of hostilities, the men of Butler's Rangers were driven from their American properties and given Royal land grants in Canada. They settled with their families as United Empire Loyalists in the Niagara Region of Ontario. The composer's wife, Susan Macpherson (née Parnall), has several Butler's Rangers ancestors.

Frederich Wilhelm Augustus von Steuben

Baron von Steuben
(1730-1794)
Charles Willson Peale, c. 1782
Oil on canvas. 20 × 23 in

Major General Frederich Wilhelm Augustus von Steuben was born of a military family in Magdeburg, Prussia, in 1730. As a young man he served as a junior officer in the Prussian Army against France during the Seven Years War in Europe, and then for a short time as an aide-de-camp to Frederick the Great.

Rumored disgraced in some obscure court scandal, he later applied to Thomas Jefferson and Silas Deane in Paris for an officer's commission in the fledgling Continental army. These men, noting his military experience and useful leadership qualities, deliberately misrepresented him to the Continental Congress as having been a Prussian lieutenant general. In 1778 he was commissioned a major general and George Washington had him appointed inspector general of his troops.

Many of the American colonists were good individual hunters and fighters, but they lacked experience in elemental military drills and in the ability to work together tactically. This circumstance had cost them defeat at the more formalized European-style skirmishes at Brandywine Creek and Germantown. After those two battles, the Prussian mercenaries found them demoralized in their winter camp at Valley Forge. Von Steuben and his military staff were then able to train them into an effective fighting force.

During that winter of training, von Steuben also wrote *Regulations for the Order and Discipline of the Troops of the United States*, which remained the official manual until 1812.

General von Steuben fought alongside Lafayette in the successful Virginia campaign of 1781 and finally commanded one of Washington's three divisions at the siege of Yorktown.

He retired to a 16,000-acre estate near Utica given to him by the people of the state of New York and died there in 1794. The small industrial city of Steubenville, Ohio, is named in his honor.

Slow March   # DIE WANDERNDEN PREUSSEN   PM H. Macpherson

MM60 (Second and third lines are harmonies — Recommended ratio 3:2:1)

EIGHTEENTH-CENTURY AMERICA

Old Ironsides

USS *Constitution*

The forty-four-gun USS *Constitution* was one of six warships authorized by President George Washington in 1797. Its purpose was primarily to protect American merchant vessels from attacks by Barbary Coast pirates from what is now Algeria and Libya. When they had been part of the British Empire, American merchantmen had been shielded from the depredations of these Arab corsairs by an annual ransom paid to the pirates from the British government; but when the American Revolution was ultimately successful, that protection ceased. As well, the Royal Navy had a habit of stopping American merchantmen on the high seas to "shanghai" their sailors for impressed service aboard British men-o'-war.

The *Constitution* put to sea in 1798 and after 207 years still continues today in US naval service. It is the oldest commissioned warship afloat in the world.

In the way of such things, then as now, the initial cost was to be $115,000, but in the end it cost $302,700. The business agent was General Henry Jackson, the construction was supervised at Edmund Hartt's Boston shipyard by Colonel George Claghorne, and its brass fittings were purchased from Paul Revere.

During the War of 1812, while engaging and eventually sinking HMS *Guerriere* 600 miles off Boston, a seaman watched a British shot bounce off its side, which was three inches thicker than the standard eighteen, and the name "Old Ironsides" was born. During that war it also captured three British men-o'-war — HMS *Pictou*, *Cyane*, and *Levant*.

Famous visitors aboard Old Ironsides have included poet Lord Byron, Pope Pius IX, and Queen Elizabeth, accompanied by Prince Philip. As late as July 2000, still operating under its own sails, it led the Parade of Sail into her home port of Boston Harbor.

Waltz
OLD IRONSIDES
PM H. Macpherson

Reel **YORKTOWN** PM H. Macpherson

The Siege of Yorktown

Impressed with the American military's success at Saratoga, the French joined the war against Britain in February 1778. In May 1781, Lord Cornwallis moved his forces to Virginia, establishing a headquarters at Yorktown on 7 August 1781, because the harbor provided easy communication with both the Royal Navy and the British commander in chief, Newfoundlander General Sir Henry Clinton.

On 28 September 1781, General Washington, aided by substantial French ground forces, besieged Lord Cornwallis and his 7,000-strong British garrison inside Yorktown. After an unsuccessful escape attempt, Lord Cornwallis surrendered on 19 October, ending the American War of Independence.

Strathspey   # THE LOUISIANA PURCHASE   PM H. Macpherson

The Louisiana Purchase

In 1803 Napoleon Bonaparte gave up on his plan to use the huge tract of land in North America given to him by his Spanish allies. At the same time, American farmers from the states to the east of the Mississippi were upset that the French port of New Orleans, controlling the mouth of the Mississippi River, was periodically shut to them, preventing them from shipping their produce down the river for sale abroad. President Thomas Jefferson sent emissaries to Paris with instructions to offer ten million dollars to purchase the southern city. To their amazement, they were instead offered Louisiana for fifteen million dollars.

At a cost of three cents per acre, the new United States of America bought not just the city, but also 828,000 square miles of territory bounded on the east by the Mississippi River, from New Orleans all the way to Duluth, and to the west by the foothills of the Rocky Mountains. This massive land mass stretched from what is now southern Alberta to northern Texas, doubling in a flash the territory of the United States.

PART THREE

Contemporary American Compositions

Slow March — **CONNIE JEAN** — Colonel Richard Adams

March — **TENOR'S DELIGHT** — Colonel Richard Adams

PATCH BARRACKS

March — Colonel Richard Adams

COLONEL RICHARD A. ADAMS, PHD, USAF (RETIRED) first received his piping instruction in Omaha, Nebraska, in the City of Omaha Pipe Band, then in Dayton, Ohio. Later, he served a four-year tour of duty at Headquarters, US European Command near Stuttgart, Germany. He traveled over 100 miles each way to practice and play with Canadian Forces Europe Pipes and Drums in Lahr under the direction of the author. Here he met his wife, Heather, who was a highland dancer with the band. Further postings found him playing with the City of Alexandria Band in Virginia and then briefly as pipe major of the City of Honolulu Band in Hawaii. Upon his return, he rejoined the City of Alexandria Band, as well as helping Dr. Ray Scott for a year with the Mary Washington College Eagle Pipe Band.

March   **THE 'K' BIRL**   PM Sandy Keith

SANDY KEITH learned to play at eleven years old at the Glasgow College of Piping. His first teacher was S. MacNeill, but he spent many hours with B. Hardie, J. Garroway, C. Scott, and A. MacNeill. He studied *piobaireachd* under Peter MacLeod. At seventeen, he immigrated to Canada, where he competed in open events and became a consistent prizewinner, studying under A.M. Cairns in Hamilton. He joined the Royal Canadian Air Force, spending valuable years under ex-Scots Guards pipe majors J.T. Mackenzie and G. Grant. He was pipe major of Erskine Pipe Band, leading them from Grade 3 to Grade 1. As director of the Dunedin piping program, he teaches at Dunedin Middle and High Schools, is pipe major of the Grade 2 City of Dunedin Pipe Band and teaches three other bands.

Slow March **MACPHERSON'S FAREWELL TO CROATAN** J. Turner

March **DR. MALCOLM MACPHERSON-SMITH** J. Turner

JOHN TURNER has played a major role for over thirty years in reviving Scottish fiddling and has won the National Scottish Fiddling Championship ten times. He judges and teaches while performing around the world, composing and arranging new music, and assisting others in their projects. Dr. Turner has been featured on twelve recordings and has contributed tracks to more than fifty others. He has performed for six US presidents and many other heads of state from around the world. He has composed more than 100 melodies, many of which have been recorded by others, published two books of music, and written numerous articles about traditional Scottish music. He founded and directs the Jink and Diddle School of Scottish Fiddling, bringing players of all ages to North Carolina each summer.

CONTEMPORARY AMERICAN COMPOSITIONS

March
THE LION'S MARCH
Ray Scott

MM60 (Second lines are harmony — Recommended ratio 4:1)

Hornpipe
RACHEL'S DANCE
Ray Scott

Hornpipe — **MILVER'S CHEERY DAY** — Ray Scott

RAY B. SCOTT, PHD, of the Chemistry Department at Mary Washington College, learned to play in 1965 under Tom Knowles and A. MacLeod in Woburn, playing in the Stuart Highlanders Pipe Band in Bedford. He went on to become pipe major of Cincinnati's Caledonia Pipes and Drums and the Lionheart Pipe Band in Virginia. He competed with the formidable Denny and Dunipace (later City of Washington) Pipe Band from 1991 until 1996, attending the World Championships twice. The hours of instruction he received from Vera Miller Patterson on playing for highland dancers resulted in his being in demand for contests all over the eastern US. Scott has directed the Mary Washington College Eagle Pipe Band since its inception in 1997.

Jig # KIP — Charlie Glendinning

Strathspey **THE ROOKERY** Charlie Glendinning

Strathspey **THE ROSARY** Charlie Glendinning

CHARLIE GLENDINNING started his musical life at three years old. He began on the piano, switched to the violin in fifth grade, and moved on to the bagpipe when he was a senior in high school. In 1971 he joined the Denny and Dunipace Pipe Band under Pipe Major Sandy Jones and became pipe sergeant of the band in 1972. He was pipe sergeant until 1999, when the band, now called the City of Washington Pipe Band, was Grade 2 World Champion at Glasgow. That year, he contracted a disease that affected his hearing; however, he still instructs the United States Naval Academy Pipe Band and competes as a soloist. He lives in Ashton, Maryland, with his wife, Paula, who still plays in the City of Washington Pipe Band.

March # FORT JACKSON — John Recknagel

Hornpipe # MORANGIE — John Recknagel

Jig • **IAIN MACDONALD - SOBHD*** • John Recknagel

* Scottish Offical Board of Highland Dance

JOHN RECKNAGEL learned to play the bagpipes under G. Killen in Toledo, Ohio. He went on to play with the Erskine Pipe Band of Hamilton, Ontario, under Sandy Keith, and the Clan McFarlane Pipe Band in St. Catharines, Ontario, under pipe majors Kenneth Eller and Joe Rennix. In 1994 he led the Atlanta Pipe Band to an unbeaten year, winning the US Grade 3 Championship.

Recknagel is currently on the Eastern US and Ontario judges' panels. He has published an exercise book with a CD, a dance piper's instruction manual, and a book of wedding and funeral music. He accompanies dance and teaches pipers' workshops in the southern and midwestern United States. A number of his previous compositions have appeared in various pipe music collections.

CONTEMPORARY AMERICAN COMPOSITIONS

Hornpipe # ROAD TO GRANDFATHER Jason Barth

Reel # SLASH PINE Jason Barth

Jig **THE TURNCOAT** Arranged by Jason Barth

(Adapted from the reel "Sound of Sleat" by D. MacKinnon)

JASON BARTH is a deaf piper from Ellicott City, Maryland, who learned to "hear" the instrument by touching the bass drone to his neck. His instructors included Robert Mitchell, William Muirhead and Charlie Glendinning. He is a former pipe major of the champion Grade 3 Dunloggin Pipe Band, as well as a former conservator of James Coldren's Bagpipe Music Museum, now located in the New Hampshire School of Scottish Arts at Manchester, and a member of the Piobaireachd Society since 1977. He is a psychotherapist living in Westminster, Maryland, where he continues to compete and to teach piping. He is now pipe sergeant of MacMillan-Birtles Memorial Pipe Band in Maryland near Washington.

CONTEMPORARY AMERICAN COMPOSITIONS

Waltz **MEGAN DEENEY** Scott Brainard

Slow Air **PENSÉES** Scott Brainard

Reel # SIDEWAYS DOWN THE HIGHWAY Scott Brainard

Jig # SLIP JIG 1991 Scott Brainard

SCOTT BRAINARD, after achieving open status as a highland dancer, learned to play the bagpipe from Charles Armijo while a student at the University of Arizona, and later had further instruction from Ian Whitelaw and John Higgins. Additionally, he has attended piping workshops and played with bands across the US, including the City of Mesa Pipe Band, Dunloggin Pipe Band and the Baltimore Police Emerald Society Pipes and Drums. He lives in the Baltimore-Washington corridor, where he is director of a Sylvan Learning Center and tends his cats.

When composing, Brainard prefers to let the melody drive the meter, which often results in asymmetric or highly syncopated tunes, a couple of which are published here.

Pipe Major Hugh Macpherson, CD

Born in Prince Albert, Saskatchewan, Pipe Major Hugh Macpherson learned to play the bagpipes in Saskatoon at thirteen years old. In 1964, at seventeen, he joined the Canadian Black Watch (Royal Highland Regiment) of Canada, where he served as an infantry piper with the First Battalion at Camp Gagetown, New Brunswick. In 1967 he traveled across the continent by train as a piper on the Canadian Centennial Tattoo.

Leaving the army, he moved to Ontario and worked as a daily newspaper reporter for the *St. Catharines Standard* until 1971, when he went back into the army with the Royal Canadian Regiment, Second Battalion and underwent combat leader and infantry section commander training. He served as an infantry corporal piper in New Brunswick and Cyprus.

He was privileged to attend the year-long British Army pipe majors' course at Edinburgh Castle, Scotland, and graduated first in his class in 1975.

Upon graduation he was assigned to form an air force volunteer band at Canadian Forces Base Portage la Prairie, Manitoba, after which he served as pipe major of Canadian Forces Europe at Lahr, West Germany, from 1977 to 1982.

He returned to Portage la Prairie for two years then attended one year of French language training at the Senior Leadership Academy. Following that, he was pipe major at CFB Greenwood in Nova Scotia until 1988, when he returned as pipe major of the Royal Canadian Regiment, Second Battalion. In 1990, 2RCR Pipes and Drums won the Grade 3 North American Championship at Maxville, Ontario.

From April 1992 until his retirement he served as pipe major of Air Command Pipes and Drums in Ottawa, achieving the rank of chief warrant officer in 1995 as senior pipe major of the Canadian Forces. During that period he was also personal piper to the governor general of Canada.

Pipe Major Macpherson retired in September 2000 and in 2004 earned a BA in history (Cum Laude) from the University of Ottawa.

In November 2004, he published his first book, *Pipers of the Canadian Regular Army: 1950-2000*.

He has been married since 1969 to Susan Macpherson (née Parnall) and has two married children — Iain Macpherson in Japan and Victoria Macpherson-Hayes in New York City.

NOTE ON THE COVER

Pictured on the cover is the author's 1897 Peter Henderson bagpipe. The silver- and ivory-mounted pipes are embellished with hand-engraved thistle-design sterling slides and ferrules. It was purchased in Camp Gagetown, New Brunswick, from a piper in the First Battalion, Canadian Black Watch (Royal Highland Regiment) in 1965. The fifty-dollar purchase price was meted out in ten five-dollar installments.

This instrument has more than a century of military service. It was played by a Scots Guards piper in the South African War in 1899; a Scottish emigrant piper serving in the Australian Army in the First World War; a piper of the British Black Watch in the Second World War; and by a Royal Scots piper during the Korean War. After a poker game under canvas in Korea secured its transfer, the instrument fell into Canadian hands and was played by Canadian Regular Army pipers until Pipe Major Macpherson's retirement in 2000. The pipes are now adapting to civilian life.

With the exception of South America and Antarctica, it has been played on every land mass in the world and on six of the seven oceans.

The American Tartan featured in the background of the cover is registered with the Scottish Tartans Authority as ITI No. 464. Designer John C. (Jack) Cumming, originally of Forfar, Angus, Scotland, based his design on the colors in the American flag. It was originally woven by Barbara Schaffer of Arizona and presented to US First Lady Betty Ford in 1976.

The badges across the bottom of the back cover are, from left: US Navy cap badge, US Army Fourth Infantry Division shoulder patch, US Air Force cap badge, US Army Tenth Mountain Division (Light Infantry) shoulder patch, and US Marine Corps cap badge.

A PIPER'S AMERICAN ODYSSEY
CONTEMPORARY BAGPIPE COMPOSITIONS
BOOK ONE
Pipe Major Hugh Macpherson, CD

Published by PENUMBRA PRESS
Printed and bound in Canada
Design by Mag Carson
Set in Goudy and Tiepolo
Text printed on Roland Opaque Vellum, Natural
Cover printed on Cornwall Coated

PENUMBRA PRESS

www.penumbrapress.ca